Caitlin O'Ryan is an actor and poet from Greater Manchester now living in London. She began performing poetry at the beginning of 2022 and has since headlined several of London's biggest spoken word nights including: SpitNights, Groove Verse, Poet's Palace, VERSES x Roundhouse and the international franchise 'Voices in Power'. She also performs as part of Sofar Sounds and has been commissioned by the likes of Refuge, British Heart Foundation and Amnesty International UK.

Also known for her recurring role in the hit TV show 'Outlander', her poem 'At What Point' about the cost of being a woman in today's society, has amassed over 16 million views online, culminating in her being invited onto BBC Woman's Hour. Her poems have been shared by the likes of Jameela Jamil, Natasha Bedingfield and Sarah Cox. Caitlin also hosts her own podcast called 'Have You Got Your Sh*t Together?', which is a celebration of not having your sh*t together. Guests include notable poets, musicians, politicians and actors.

at what point

caitlin o'ryan

Illustrated by Emily Treloar

Burning Eye

BurningEyeBooks
Never Knowingly
Mainstream

This edition published by Burning Eye Books 2025

www.burningeye.co.uk

@burningeyebooks

Burning Eye Books
15 West Hill, Portishead, BS20 6LG

ISBN 978-1-913958-50-3
Cover photographs by George Lawrence @triggercrappy
Emboidery by Katie Pickering @kt_stitchworks
Illustrations by Emily Treloar @emilyruthtreloar

for mum & dad: for your love, support, belief and sacrifices.

for Liadhan: my first audience member, director and genuine laugh.

Bright and fierce and fickle is the South,
And dark and true and tender is the North.

Alfred, Lord Tennyson

Wherever you go, you'll meet yourself.

Gran

Caveat

The majority of these poems were written to be
read aloud; I hope they translate to page.

They were written by someone with
a Northern accent.

The order of the poems is somewhat chronological.
Feel free to dip in and out, or to read start to
finish, and join me on the emotional rollercoaster
of my twenties.

If I die, and all I've known is poetry
Well, maybe that's enough for me

me?
shit
shit together

Introduction

'At what point will I feel like I've got my shit together?' I asked my dad, having escaped back home to Oldham after my first breakup.

I was twenty-four years old, had just moved to London and was two years into navigating a career as an actor where unpredictability and rejection were beginning to feel like the only reliable constants in my life. Everything else seemed coloured by impermanence.

This was not what I had been sold as a kid. I remember sitting in classrooms, zoning out of triple maths and escaping into daydreams where I would imagine the adult I would one day become. It's not that I had a particular vision for the future – I'm not sure I've ever longed for the picket fence, white wedding, 2.4 children – but it was more the feeling it gave me. The sense of calm. The knowledge that, no matter how awful I felt about myself in school, I would, at some point, be an adult who drove a car and owned a house. And adults who drive cars and own houses have their shit together.*

So, back in Oldham, staring expectantly into my dad's eyes, I was horrified to hear that:

a) that probably isn't going to happen any time soon, and
b) he still feels like a twenty-one-year-old who wakes up every morning and tries to make it through the day the best he can.

Cool.

My twenties have been a constant confrontation of things I took as certainties being called into question, of mirrors smashing and of being forced to accept the reality of an insecure life. No one prepares you for this. It might have been nice if, instead of teaching us trigonometry, somebody had sat us down and said:

---

* Spoiler: I do not own a house and cannot (legally) drive a car

'Hey, being an adult is actually really hard and, at times, it will feel like a complete shitshow. You'll feel happy and sad and lonely and scared, and you'll also see your loved ones feeling happy and sad and lonely and scared and not really know what to do with it, but you'll suddenly feel very responsible. You'll see your parents' flaws and fallibilities, and that's weird. You're probably going to rent forever and the job market is fucked and dating apps make people treat you like commodities and everything is moving so fast that you'll feel like you can't breathe sometimes and you'll be terrified of being left behind and it'll make you constantly anxious and the world is literally burning and fascism will start to make a comeback and, girls – they're coming for your rights again! They'll make you feel personally responsible for it all, but also that you have zero power to do anything about it, so what's the point anyway? But, hey, at least you'll know your way around a triangle!'

Also, tax returns. I wish they had sat us down and taught us how to do those.

I guess there is no blueprint. There is no guide to navigating these years. If I hadn't had to experience heartbreak/grief/anger/fear head-on, would I have grown as a person? I'm not sure; I certainly wouldn't have written as many poems.

These moments force you to meet yourself, to confront things about yourself and to figure out the kind of person you want to be in this world. They break you and they (hopefully) remake you.

I write poetry because it helps me to process all of these things. When nothing feels tangible, I cling desperately to words in the hope that they'll allow me to gather the elusive and distil them into something real. Something to grab hold of and feel some semblance of control over.

Poetry is empathy; it is pure connection and understanding. A gateway into someone's inner world and emotions. It is catharsis and community, a way of relating to each other that says, *You are not alone; I also feel this.* It is a shared humanity.

The year I release this poetry collection, I will have just turned thirty. I will still be feeling quite lost and staring into an uncertain future, both personally and politically, but I will be taking with me a load of learnings, incredible friendships, a heapful of joyful memories and a whole lot of love.

This collection, then, feels like an opportunity to take stock. To collate the poems I have written throughout this last decade, and to organise them into some kind of time capsule. A homage to this chapter of my life, in which the recurring question has been 'At what point…?'

If you have bought this book, thank you. The fact my words have resonated with so many is still pretty mad to me. These are poems I have written in various bedrooms scattered across London, on (delayed) train rides back up North, tube journeys to and from gigs and late-night buses home. They are poems about love, heartbreak, healing, rage, fear, friendship and joy. They were written out of necessity. They are personal to me and my own experiences. But, if you can see yourself within my poems, that means that we share something. Something deeper than the latest trends or what the algorithms prescribe to us. We share a perspective, a lived experience, a universal truth. We are connected, you and I, and I think that's pretty special in a world that can feel so isolating.

I hope my words can bring you comfort. Something to grab hold of and to call your own. A *'you are not alone; I also feel this.'*

So, **at what point** do I let go of these poems and **at what point** do they become yours?

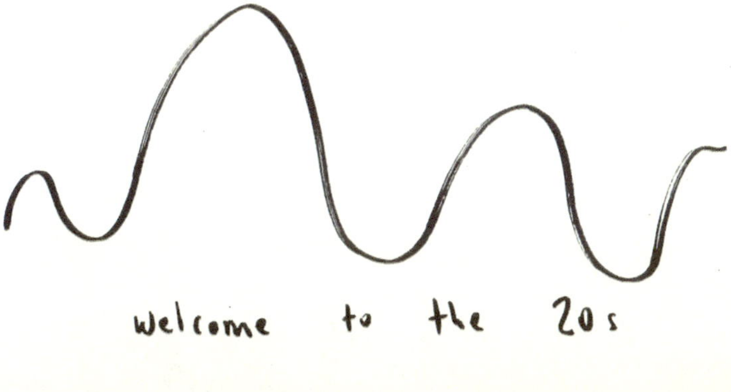

Contents

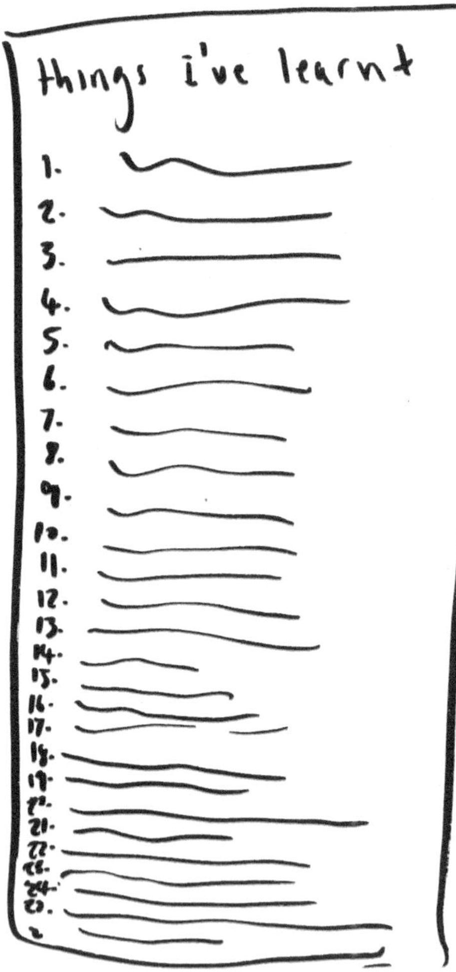
things i've learnt

Things I've Learnt So Far

Late twenties is not *that* old;
you will both appreciate and lament this upon reaching it.
The things you took as certainties
when you imagined your 'mature' late twenties
will be ever-shifting markers in the ground.
You will tell yourself that you still have time,
you're still finding yourself.
It's fine that you don't have
a house,
a partner,
a steady job
or financial security.
Take the pressure off!
You are not your parents' generation
and the Tories have fucked us all.

Relationships will come and go
and you will know yourself all the better in the interim.
Technology both terrifies and excites you;
you are old enough to remember a life before it
but young enough that considering a life without it
feels nigh on impossible.
You will judge people who post for likes
and then be secretly gutted when your posts don't get enough likes.

You will learn what a 'fuckboy' is and how to spot one.
You may still yearn for the rollercoaster from time to time,
but you'll come to realise there's a beauty that lies
within somebody who is able to emotionally self-regulate.

You will have forgotten most of your early memories,
the ones you couldn't comprehend losing as a child,
but smells will bring them back randomly
like a slap in the face
and you'll laugh

and think how weird it is, being a human.
You'll cry over freshly mown grass,
rejoicing in the lighter nights after a relentless winter.

You will see your parents getting older and it will scare you,
maybe even anger you.
You'll feel a sense of betrayal at discovering their fallibility,
but one day, you might be able to see it as a beautiful thing,
and it will make you feel closer to them.

You will realise
that you cannot run away from your own problems
by determining to fix somebody else's.
Stop hiding behind their chaos.
Your ability to give your friends therapy
will not mean you have completed your own.
Self-help books will not fix your broken heart;
it is another form of distraction.
You must sit with it,
roll amongst the shit with it,
and then you must dust yourself off and carry on.

All of your friends will be sad.
There will come a time when it will feel like
everyone you love is struggling.
It will be overwhelming,
like small fires everywhere.
You'll question why no one warned you of the constant anxiety
that accompanies your twenties.
You'll see loved ones submerge and fight to stay afloat.
You can throw them a rope
but you cannot make them take hold.
Learning this will save you a great deal of time and energy.

You will feel like the world is imploding on itself
and you will teeter between anger and rage and protest
and shrugs of apathy
and an acceptance of impending doom.
You will question why anyone is having children anymore

but fear that without them, you will die alone.
You will drink.
You will give it up.
You will drink again,
and sometimes you will smoke,
but you will lie about it to your doctor
and wonder if your dentist can read it on your teeth.

You will likely have experienced loss;
it comes in different forms.
It's okay to be as upset about losing your dog
as someone else is about their grandma;
it fucking sucks.
Your grief is your own.
Feel no shame in how it manifests
or how it pops up randomly on a Tuesday in a café
when a certain song comes on.

Make time for active rest.
You will worry about the amount you worry
and vow to worry less.
You will remember what Cher said
on that episode of Graham Norton you watched a few years ago:
If it doesn't matter in five years, it doesn't matter.
You will strive to be more like Cher.

Share your life.
Only a fool plays it cool.
Lean in;
after all,
on your deathbed
you won't regret having told someone that you liked them
or having gushed over someone who inspires you.
You *will* regret all the flowers you were too afraid to give
and the fact that you won't be able to 'dance like no one's watching'
when you're dead
and there is
in fact
no one watching.

Everything you want is on the other side of fear,
so bite the fucking bullet and do it anyway.

But go easy on yourself.
The world has enough bullies;
don't become your own.
If you spoke to your mates like you do to yourself
you'd have no mates,
and you need your mates.
You need your people.
Life is all about the people.

But nobody likes a people pleaser.

Learn to say 'no'.
It will be hard,
but you will come to realise
it is a full fucking sentence

and with that you will go far.

Friends from Towns

a poem about trying to find your feet in a big, fast-paced, anonymous city

Friends from towns are settling down:
lifelong partners,
sourdough starters,
talking wedding dresses,
and I'm impressed they managed to get a mortgage;
it's more than I can manage
to get up in the morning
after late nights out.

Feeling like death with a debt to pay.
Flat whites are drinking my savings away,
and, in this lonely city,
though we're made of millions strong,
isn't it a pity
that love keeps going wrong?
Passing ships in the night,
desperate to make the right decisions,
clinging to perfection
in this mess that we call living.
Chasing the dream
in a thousand various directions,
I can't commit to sleep, let alone to deep connections.
Call it self-protection:
if it's not *instant*
it's not for me,
unless, of course, I'm talking about my one-a-day coffee.
You can keep your granules.
(I may not have much,
but I'll always have standards.)

I'm wanting cool, Instagrammable spaces
that famous names and faces implore I should 'check out'.
I'm decking out my rented pad
with plants I can't keep satisfied,

hiding from responsibilities
with too little water or too much light;
it's hard to get the balance right.
These bricks I'll never own.
This house will never be my home,
and it seems the only thing I can invest in
is men with complex issues,
the 'sure, let me try and fix you's.

And it's frightening
how solitude is tightening its grip,
how quickly we can slip
into filling up with things we lack,
stuffing holes to hide the cracks.

I'm playing invisible Twister and insufficiency is the spinner.
I'm here, I'm there, I'm everywhere
and then I'm racing home for dinner,
and by that I mean my *tea*.
My God, this city will take it all from me,
including my Northern identity.

I'm constantly tired
but constantly bored.
I constantly feel like I'm being ignored.
When I need some connection there's nobody there,
when I need privacy suddenly people stare.
I'm constantly guilty;
it's never enough.
I constantly wish I felt a little less rough.

The streets are paved with gold,
and when I'm older
I'll make time to rest.
But when I'm older and I'm past my best
will I regret not settling sooner?
The longing as opposed to living?
The take, take, taking as opposed to giving in,
to riding the ride of this thing we call life,

the 'settling down' and the 'being the wife'?
I'm rallying against the expected,
but will I regret the rejected opportunities for simplicity?
The house, the dog, the you and me,
the baby, the garden, the growing old comfortably?

Time will tell.
But till then, please tell me
that
I
still
have
time.

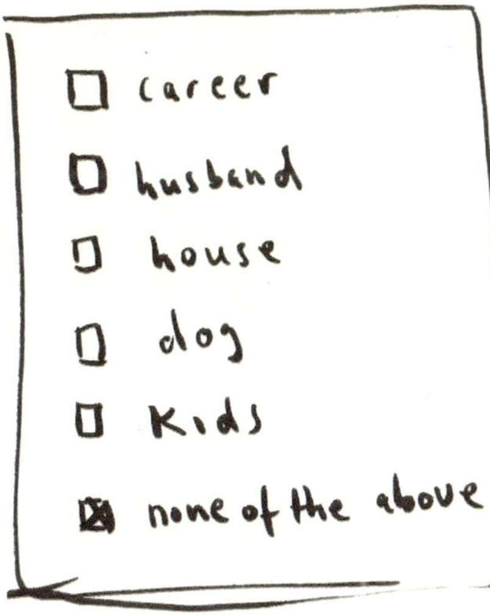

When It Comes to Sobriety

When it comes to sobriety
I'm a bit of a mess.
I find it hard to confess my feelings
unless I'm dancing on the ceiling.
Quite literally,
I'm a liability,
a disaster fuelled by G&Ts,
waking up with swollen knees
and bruises I don't remember collecting
for people I don't remember protecting
or provoking.

It's paradoxical,
this concoctional feeling of reeling and rolling around
yet with both feet firmly on the ground
most of the time.

Voddy soda and fresh lime?
You're making yours a double?
I'll do the same to mine!

Shots? Fuck, yes!
I've had a stressful week.
I'm tired of feeling lonely.
It's boring feeling bleak.

There's a fine line that tips me
from *tipsy*
to twat,
but that's hard to see
when I'm already cracking out the next bottle of wine,
topping up yours so that you'll top up mine.

We're escaping the monotony,
the forgotten grey of days that play on repeat
for five out of seven days of the week.
I'm feeling pent up and I'm ready to pop.
This fizzing inside, once it starts, it can't stop.

We're in this together;
we ride and die.
And when we wake up,
all tender and shy,
we'll lie we can't remember
the states that we were in,
that it wasn't *that* embarrassing
when you threw up in that bin,
and we'll swear that that's the last time
until the week begins again.

Counting down the days now,
I'm lost amongst the maze now
of dead-end jobs and football mobs,
reasoning with Karen bobs,
pretending to care whilst inside something throbs for change.

I hope I can change.
I hope it's not like this forever.

Today

written whilst working in one of many hospitality jobs

Today
I served a toddler
Who asked for a babyccino
With marshmallows
And chocolate dusting on top

Today
I watched
As a woman gave birth on the news underground
As they hid
Waiting
For the bombings to stop

Today
I served an old man
Who came in to use the toilet
And ordered a coffee while he waited
He was humiliated
When I told him we no longer accept cash
Don't get old
He whispered to me
Through embarrassed bleary eyes
As he reluctantly returned the pounds to his pocket
The only change he has any control over

Today
A woman complained
Because her cheese wasn't melted enough
Whilst tents in Gaza were aflame

Today
People with prams tutted loudly about the tube strikes
As a moleish man I had never met before
Sat at the counter
Sipping his coffee in daylight for the first time
As he left
He returned the cup and said

Sorry about the strikes
But they're taking our pensions, you see

Instead of Bras I'm Setting Twitter* Alight

a poem about performative activism

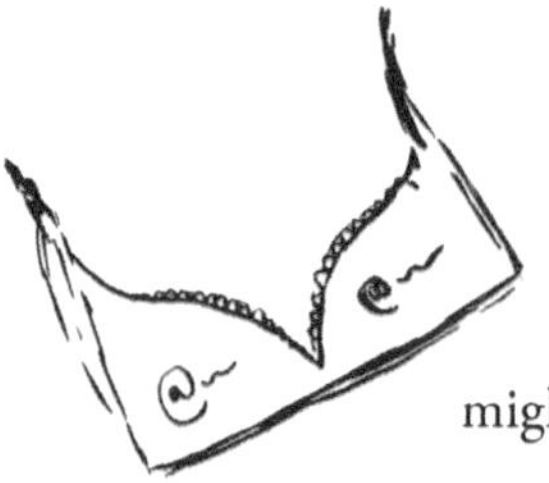

Instead of bras
I'm setting my Twitter alight.
A provocative tweet that, if written right,
might ruffle the feathers of followers unfavoured,
who'll swiftly unfollow
right after they've savoured
the opportunity to proudly pronounce their distaste:
a loud reply laced with
obnoxious contempt and a scattering of scorn,
an attempt by them to publicly thorn my opinion
and deflate my views
or simply dismiss me 'cause they can't see past the boobs.

And I'll convince myself that I've made a difference,
that for every unfollow there'll be someone who's listening
and that my little tweet might reach about ten
who, if they should retweet,
will help to stem that idea into a branch,
and my little tweet might be given the chance
to enter more feeds and attract more thumbs.

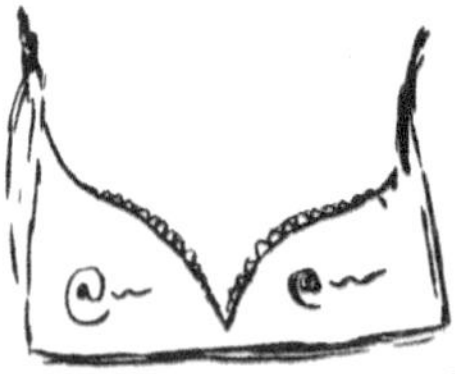

To rise up out of the gutter,
away from the slums
and into the mainstream,
where teams of people will take up arms
and rejoice in their leader they read in their palms
who awoke them from their scrolling slumbers
and through their awakening drove them out in their numbers.
Trickling through streets,
becoming a tide
to wash out the bourgeois,
overturning the times,

---

* I'll never call it X. Sorry.

taking back powers for what we hold dear.
No room for racist climate-change deniers here.
Out with you sexist, sceptical preachers,
you liars, you thieves,
you power-hungry leeches.
For too long we've let you fight over the reins.
Now your horsemen are here and we're demanding change.
You set fire to our home,
tore our country apart.
Enough is enough.
We want a fresh start.

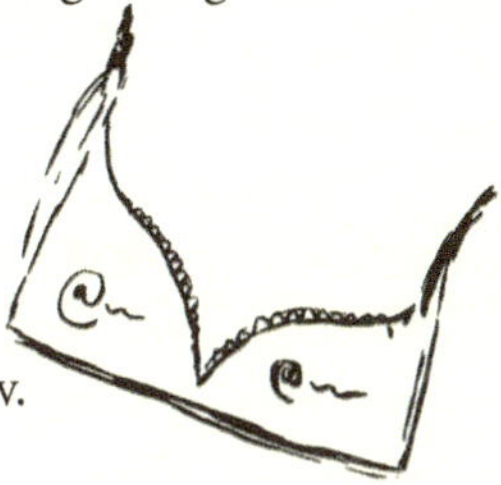

And from out of the rubble a phoenix will grow.
In pyjamas and slippers our unlikely hero
will flip-flop up to the soapbox stand,
groggy,
bemused,
phone in hand,
branded forever as the 'freedom fighter'
whose little tweet pulled a viral overnighter
that spoke to the hearts of so many people
and asked not for power, but for all to be equal.
An inspiration for a redundant generation
who barely recognise their home.
Proof you *can* change the world –
all you need is your phone.

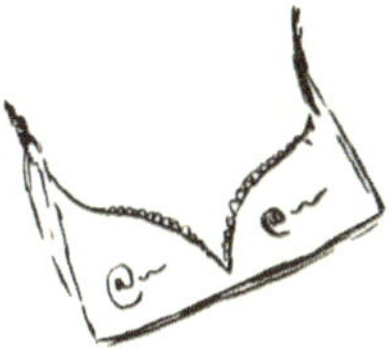

I step forward to address the adoring cheers
but am struck by the realisation I'm not the only one here.
There are hundreds now jostling to take control of the mic,
thousands of others setting their phones alight,
but with so many choices
and so much white noise
it's impossible to distinguish a single voice.
Blending together a blur of dissatisfaction,
an offended, lethargic way of taking action.

Thumbs fire like bullets out into the aether,
drawing out of the shadows a tempestuous creature
that feeds on confusion and indecision,
pouncing when it picks up on potential divisions.
Snarling, it circles but comes to a standstill,
its eyes overwhelmed by what it sees in this land filled with anger and pain,
poverty and pride,
a nation abetting its own suicide.
Satisfied, the creature slinks back to its cell.
What more can I do? They're destroying themselves.

Hovering, my thumb gently presses the send,
preparing myself for this riot I penned.
A whole day I wait, so that I can really savour it.
Some notifications.
I click:

One retweet.
One favourite.

Pretending to Talk

will they, won't they

Pretending to talk
With neither one listening
Static tingles
Between every positioning
We shouldn't be here
It's been years since we were
Everything's different
We know this can't work
It's not in what we say
It's in what we don't ask
Struggling to move on
Because we're focused on the past
The past will pass us by
Overlap us in a second
If we don't act
On what has always threatened
Plenty to win

But all the more to lose
And so we both refuse
To be the one responsible for choosing
Wrong or right
So we lie there past midnight
Frozen but alive
Fizzing side by side
Breaths shallow
Eyes closed
The minutes pass by
Suspended in our pose
Never so aware
Of every contour of our being
Knowing any minor movement
Might send this moment fleeing

I Wanna Bake a Cake

I wanna bake a cake
And I want it to be shit
I wanna get distracted
'Cause I think you're really fit
Put in too much flour
Mix the sugar with the salt
I want a heated conversation
About the fact that it's your fault
I wanna stick it in the oven
And for you to pull me tight
I wanna rub your hands all over me
Not caring if it's right
I want a soggy bottom
I want a pancake with no rise
And if it comes out alright
I want us both to be surprised
I don't want Ottolenghi
Or some Mary Berry kit
I just wanna bake a cake
And I want it to be shit

I Love You Like a Brother

for when loving someone isn't enough

this was the first ever poem I performed at an open mic. I had just gone through my first proper breakup and, like with all good breakups, I wrote a poem about it in my notes app that I felt needed exorcising

I burst into tears straight after x

I love you like a brother;
that motherly kind of love that's unconditional.
I'll catch you any time you fall.
If there's a wall
I'll be the one pushing you up from below,
so that you can grow
high enough to pull yourself over,
to stand tall and conquer.

I will always have your back,
never lack in positive things to say about you;
you are all fairy tales come true.

What I'd do
to be half the human you are:
your kindness knows no bounds,
no flaws I've found in your compassionate advice,
you make me think twice about rash decisions,
ground me during fearful visions
of my future and my past,
you really make me laugh,
you're good at being daft and building me back up
from nothing,
you're really something,
and I love you for that.

But that love isn't right
and, try as I might,
I can't force those feelings to come,
to let go and succumb
when you hold me
and try to mould me.
So I'm holding back what I'm really thinking,
because if it starts to sink in
I know there's no way back for us;
it'll be the end of trust.

Maybe I'm being selfish,
but I want you in my life forever,
so the thought of nevermore
keeps my jaw firmly sealed
and these thoughts I must shield
until I'm ready to face how life was before I met you.
And you gave me everything you possibly could,
and I took it
and I kept it safe,
but now all your giving is becoming a weight,
something I know is good for me
but something that I hate
because, try as I might,
I can't reciprocate.

I want for you what's best,
but it's hard to confess that that may not be me.
It's hard to see an alternative reality
where you're no longer mine,
where time has come between us
and, like scenes from a dusty film,
our memories, once sensitive and raw,
become almost impossible to recall.

Where someone else is now your other,
someone else receives that love that felt so unmistakably me-shaped.
So, inexplicably, we
are becoming strangers to each other,
and together we have smothered
one another from our light,
sucked the oxygen from our candles so we no longer burn bright.
Frightened to convey what we're really feeling:
no longer does *forever* sound particularly appealing.
Concealing the nagging notions we can't seem to silence
that started off small but crescendoed to sirens.

Maybe it's a testament to our affection and devotion
that we've stayed in this thing, just going through the motions.

Oceans form behind both of our eyes.
Who was it that said there's no good in goodbyes?
Your hand sits in mine for what could be the last time,
clammy and nails bitten,
about to turn the page on this story that we've written.
It's not quite the ending that we both had in mind,
but that doesn't mean we haven't had
the fucking time of our lives.

I look into your eyes,
an unforgettable blue,
stroke your hair and whisper that I will always love you.
And in that moment we're nineteen again,
content with being two,
and, darling,
I'll never whisper anything so true.

There's a Place

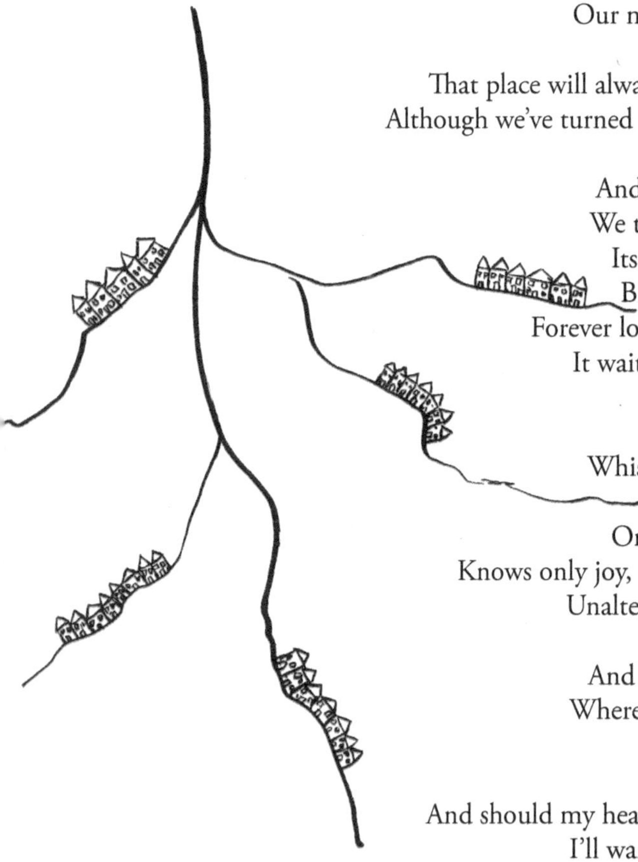

There's a place
Where we still roam
Our memories etched
Into its bones
That place will always be our home
Although we've turned our backs on us

And in those streets
We trickled through
Its veins still bleed
Both me and you
Forever loyal, forever true
It waits for our return

There's a place
Whispers our names
As if we're still
One and the same
Knows only joy, nothing of pain
Unaltered in our wake

And on those streets
Where we once kissed
Our glory days
Always exist
And should my heart begin to miss
I'll wander for a while

As I Pull Into the Station

And as I pull into the station
I am faced
With ghosts of you and I
Embracing
Me returning
From some far-off place and
You awaiting
Patiently
I wonder who you wait for now
Weaving through the waiting halves
I think I see your face
But then again, that's nothing new

Did You Drink Coffee?

Did you drink coffee the next day?
Maybe with a cigarette,
breathing in the morning air?
I remember it was dry
that day back in July.

Did you have a shower?
Maybe at the same time as mine,
the water dripping down our synchronised spines.
I stared as my hair spiralled down the plughole.
I don't know why that's what stayed with me
about that morning in July.

I drank a lot of orange juice.
I didn't really want it,
but my friend had gone out specially
that morning and had bought it.
He wanted to help,
and I wanted him to know that I was grateful,
so I downed it
as he handed me yet another plateful
of toast
that I'd leave to go cold.

Did you ever find my earring?
It was one of my favourites.
I'd bought it from Accessorize
upon receiving my first payment
from the job that I had hated
whilst my mates all went to uni.
I doubt you would have kept it.
I guess it didn't mean anything to you.

Did you go to a beer garden and bask in the sun?
Maybe we were at parallel tables in the same one.
I had a Rekorderlig; I don't drink them anymore.
I can't remember buying it.
I can remember watching as a fly slowly died in it
and I wondered whose fault it was,
the cider or the fly's,
that day back in July.

Yes Is Complex

a poem exploring the complexities around consent and the often-undiscussed power dynamics

*this was one of the first of my poems that people really connected with, leading to me getting booked for my first headline slot**

It's more than a *yes* or a *no*.
It's a feeling that tingles through bones,
that signals the tone
for how the evening might go.

I know
it's a grey area,
but it's a great area to be in:
the anticipation,
the static vibrations,
the electricity of you and me,
the back and forth of who will be
the first to crack and succumb to temptation.

It's fire.
It's light.
It's a moment that leaves your chest feeling tight
with the pounding of hearts and the *who's gonna starts.*
It's invisible,
but it's *present.*
It's tangible and it presents
a moment that will resonate and relegate
time and space
to meaningless circumstances.
We've both taken chances
and our bodies will dance to a rhythm we've created
through the language they speak
silently to each other.

* Thank you, Memo Brown and SAYS Events.

It's more than an utter of *yes* or *no*.
It's the quiet untold.
It's the energy we hold.

I can say *yes*, but my stance might say *no*.
I can say *yes* but might really want you to go.
I know
it's confusing
and, fuck, it's frustrating,
and I can't tell you how many times I've ended up hating myself
for making myself
go along with situations
I am not entirely comfortable with.

Because I worry how *no* might be received.
It's so much easier for me to people-please.
Appeasing comes easily to me,
it's my safe space, because I have seen
the alternative.

I've had to alter my behaviour due to 'ulterior learning'.
I've had to educate myself in your unspoken yearnings.
If I can read the unwritten, why aren't *you* observing
the subtleties I'm trying to suggest,
the *no* my body screams as you start to undress?

I know
I should just say *no*,
but sometimes there's nowhere for that *no* to go.
I know how that *no* might quickly unfold.
I know how that *no* might lead you to scold
with accusations
and unwanted confrontations,
and so I resignate myself to a place of placation.

Here's an education:
if it's not a *fuck, yes!* it's a *no*.
If I hesitate or say, 'Erm, sure...' you should go.
If I say that I'm tired you should know what that means.

If I'm drunk you should not be unbuckling your jeans.
No, I'm not being coy just to make you more keen.
No will always mean *no,*
but *yes* is complex.

I know
you're confused,
'cause you think that by asking you're letting me choose,
but I know what *might* happen if I was to refuse.
So, if I can't say *no*,
then what's left?
If I can't say *no*,
is that a *yes?*

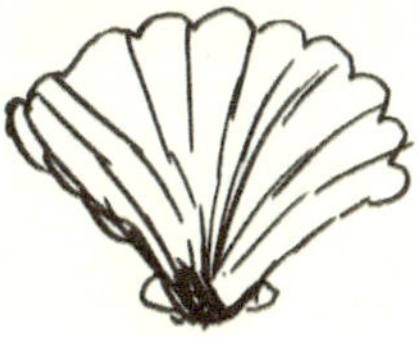

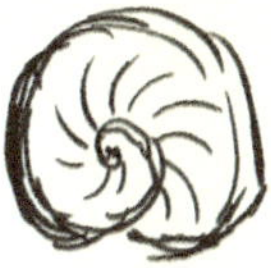

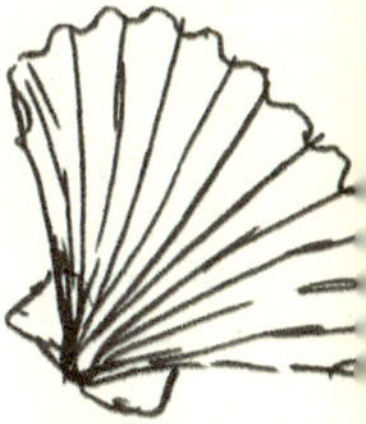

My Head Is in Your Lap

for my Anglesey pals; you are my constants

My head is in your lap
Whilst you natter
Passing picky bits
As laughter
Punctuates your chat
And in your cadence I drift off
Carried far from anxious thoughts
Your fingers comb through hair
And there is nowhere else I'd rather be
Than with my friends down by the sea

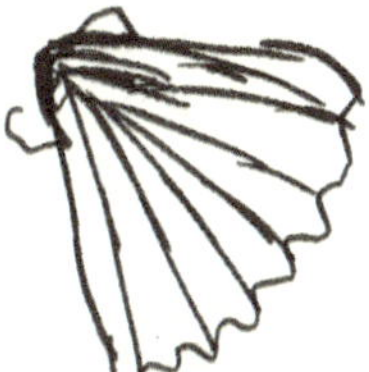

Ode De Toilette

dedicated to all the wonderful womxn I have encountered there

I have fallen in love
with so many women
in the toilets of clubs
and bars and restaurants.
I've put the world to rights
with strangers I'll never know the names of,
these drunken angels
in the refuge of the restroom.
If heaven has gates,
may they be adorned with a golden 'F'
or the outline of a figure in dress.

I've pressed my lips against the temple
of a girl gone existential
as she stares upon her own reflection
and projects the universal question:
Am I good enough?
Tears tracking down her face,
I replace with compliments passed on to me
from other women
who came before me,
who have stood where I stand now
in high heels and trainers,
these feminist trailblazers:

You've got this, girl!
Or, *You're amazing!*
Or, *Your tits look fucking great in that!*

And for a moment we are equal,
and for a moment we all mean it.
A backstage world where women can breathe
without performing for the eyes that decide how we're seen,
and there's no competition;

we're joint in our mission
to gas each other up.
A brief interlude
to debrief and collude,
swap war stories in loos
and check in with each other.

A quick wee and therapy?
That's two birds with one stone.
In the cubicle next to me?
That's two birds and one's stoned;
I can hear them chatting shit
and I'm fucking here for it.

It can be chaos,
it can be cathartic,
it can be the best place to be at a party –
a much-needed timeout
overlooked by London's *Time Out.*
An *if you know, you know,*
and we all know
why it takes a woman so long to go
to the toilet.
It's because it's so much *more* than a toilet.
It's a place for her to let her hair down
just for a second
before having to collect herself again
and carry the weight of the world
in her clutch or her handbag.
We'll top her up
when the world tears her down,
make sure her makeup is in place
so she can bear to face it again.

That's why the place is so packed
and the queues are so long.
Our bladders may be weak,
but my god, the vibes are strong.

Pressure

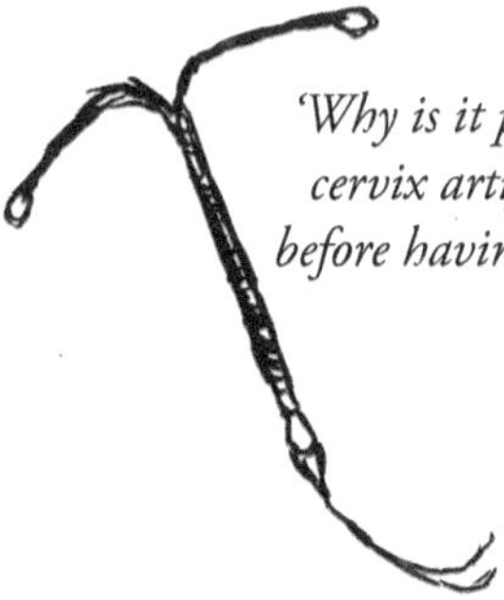

'Why is it presumed that women will be fine with having their cervix artificially dilated with a pair of metal barbecue tongs before having what is basically the wire coat hanger from a doll's house inserted into their uterus?'
Caitlin Moran

It just feels like such a pressure for me
He says
A pressure
He says
A pressure to be with me

Sure
I don't say
I don't say how the pressure felt
Going in
How it lingered
How I couldn't feel my fingers
From squeezing my knuckles so tight
How the light stained my eyes
As I stared at a spot on the polystyrene ceiling
Wishing myself devoid of feeling

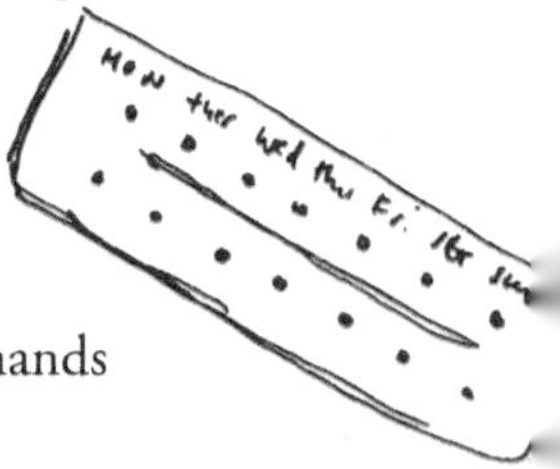

A pressure
He says
When I'd lain on a bed
Alone
With prying eyes and foreign hands
Not consented female's
But unexplained man's
Who'd watched me as I'd removed my layers
Who'd watched me as I'd whispered prayers
To a god I'd long forgotten
Whilst they swabbed at me with sticks of cotton
And in the silence held me still
Biting lip to stop sound from spilling over

Just breathe
They sang
But my body rang with a pain
Far louder than their counting numbers
Such a barbaric encounter devoid of numbness
How my insides had writhed
With a shame I'd fought to hide
Whilst they branded me with copper T
And he
Sat outside on his phone
The pressure
Of going to Tesco all by himself
Of picking out an ice cream flavour
To try and make amends

I'd come out shaking
Could barely speak
He asked me *what happened?* but
Too weak to answer
I climbed into the car and stared straight ahead
I wasn't prepared
For the white turning red
The invasion of privacy
How much it would hurt

Just drive
I whisper
As oblivious commuting cars go past
But he fails to pull out in time
Which, ironically
Is what got us into this *pressure* in the first place

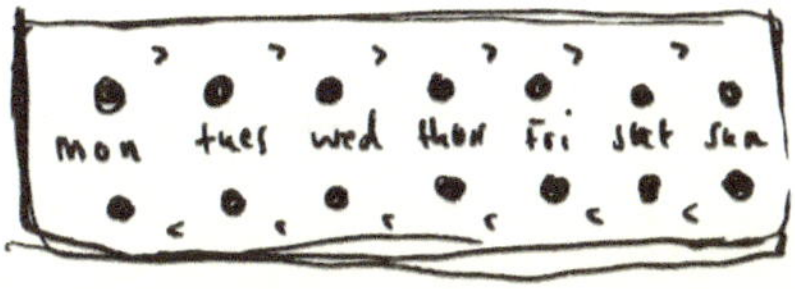

You Hate Men*

a pretty much verbatim poem about the worst date I ever went on

You
Hate
Men

he says,
sat across from me.
The menu sits between us
in the silence.

There are men out there
Who are violent
But I'm not like that
And I resent the fact
That you can't see
I resent the fact
That when you say
'Patriarchy'
You don't exclude me

You need to check yourself
I'm trying my hardest
I'm doing my best
Jesus Christ
It's like a never-ending fucking test
What more can I say?
What more can I do?
It seems like nothing's enough for you
When you say *'patriarchy'*
Do you not see
That the real victims here are the people like me?

---

* I don't

No, stop it
Now you're twisting my words
No, *stop it*
I just think it's really absurd
That you *want* a man who treats you like a piece of shit
And I'm sat here, right, and I feel like a tit
'Cause I'm a nice guy and I get overlooked
I'm a nice guy, but it's like you're expecting something *better*
to come along

No
Stop it
Wait
Can't you see that you're wrong?

I just think it's *unfair*
I think it's *complex*
I think people, yeah, they're scared to talk about sex in this way
So black and white
That they're missing the grey

Now you've got your back up, yeah
I can already see
You have, you've got your back up
Why can't we agree that there's *degrees* to this thing?

'Cause statistically, yeah
Statistically
No
Wait

Let me finish

Statistically, yeah
I'm more likely to
You know what I'm saying?
And that's statistics, yeah
I'm talking statistics

Why are you quiet?
Why aren't you saying anything?
Why aren't you looking at me?
Oh, well, now I feel bad
Don't make me feel bad

I'm sorry, alright?
I'm sorry, okay?
I'm sorry, it's just
Fuck, I don't know what to say
It's just hard, y'know?
When you're a nice guy
And it's hard, 'cause
Oh, God, please don't cry
I'm sorry, alright?
What more do you want?
I'm sorry, okay?
Maybe I am in the wrong
It's just hard, 'cause
Well, there's no one to talk to about this sort of stuff
And it's hard, 'cause
See, that's why I wanted to bring all this up
Because it's a *safe space*
And I can't talk to my mates
It's a *safe space*
C'mon, don't ruin the date

And if I'm honest, yeah
I think you handled that perfectly
And if I'm honest, yeah
See, that's why I think you're the girl for me
Because I *like* that you're strong
And don't get me wrong
But this
Is actually
The most attracted I've been to you right now

She Sits and She Drinks

She sits and she drinks another wine all on her own,
'cause at least when there's a glass within her hand she's not alone.
For, if there's one thing that's certain,
it's that another version of reality exists
beyond the bottom of this bottle.
Neither good nor bad, just numb:
what happens in the space where cognisance is undone,
where the voices surrender themselves from rumination,
vacating their heightened state of stimulation,
a place where they allow just for a moment
relaxation and rest.
Just for a moment.
Some rest,
just for a moment.

And once her lips have drained the final drops
she's past the point she'd told herself she'd stop,
for, with the best will in the world,
her ability gets hazy.
That line that seemed so clear
has somehow started to get wavy,
it's malleable and moves.
She's left with nothing left to prove,
so she'll relinquish the control,
lets the substance take its toll,
for, once it has a hold of her,
well, at least she's being held.
The loneliness of living for a moment has been quelled,
and her well that ran so empty
has been filled with something fleeting,
a wave that drags her under
before finally retreating
and leaving her
exposed.

It repels her when she's sober.
Swears this morning that it's over
as she's woken up by shame again,
the nausea and pain again.
The gaps in recollection
causing cracks in her reflection,
for there are sections of herself
she can't recall
and in the cold light of day, she'd be appalled

at the crying
and the screaming,
at the falling
and the scheming
for another secret sip of sweet escape,
careless of the warnings of the life she puts at stake,
and, with shaking clammy hands,
her subconscious makes demands,
and she's too tired to take a stand against its calling.
It offers her a comfort her discomfort finds enthralling.

And she'll stall,
she'll turn away,
but eventually that summoning will have the final say
and she'll find herself back where she was always going to start:
one hand around a bottle
and one hand across her heart.
The last time,
she'll whisper to herself so quietly,
just like the last *last time.*

And she is lost to us again,
escaped to somewhere distant:
a place she doesn't have to face the fear of her existence,
the persistence of anxiety
to which she's losing her resistance.

Her resilience is gone;
I don't know where to find it.
She's making wrong decisions,
can't work out how to rewind it.
She's running and she's running,
but her past is still behind,
it's closing in.

And no matter all the tins she downs
and cans she pounds,
when dawn comes back around
it's still herself she will be met with in the morning.

Oh, how the morning carries mourning,
'cause she can't do this any more.
Can't muster up the strength to place her feet upon the floor.
And it's getting to the point
where something has to give:
allow herself to drown
or dredge up the thirst to live.
And we can stand and throw the rope,
but it's for her to take a hold.
We can lead her to the reins,
but it's for her to take control.

Please let her go,
I whisper to this sickness in her soul.
I miss the girl I love
and her happiness you stole.

Your Heart Is Left Broken

Your heart is left broken
It's shattered around
There's pieces of you scattered sharp on the ground
You're searching for fragments that cannot be found
It's astounding to me
How someone like you could be brought to your knees
How someone like you could be struggling to breathe
With the weight of it all

But I'll wait
And I'll watch
And I'll lie by your side
I'll patiently answer those thoughts you can't hide
And as you tear yourself apart
I'll hold your tender heart
My red palms will squeeze calm into its irregularity
My soft words will soothe and bring you back to some clarity
And together we'll mend the deepest of cavities
We'll make you whole again

Time heals, and we have all the time
You chose to love, and loss is just a sign
Of your capacity to give
You were brave enough to live
You were bold enough to feel things in their entirety
So in this darkness steal a glance around
Allow yourself to revel in the light that you have found
For there's bound to be some
A glint or a glimmer
A resilient shimmer

Breathe it in and scream it out
Purge yourself of any doubt that you will rise again
When tissue mends it forms a scar
A reminder of just how strong you are
And not so far from now
Without knowing exactly how or why
You'll discover that you are ready to try again
Dip your toe in the ocean without knowing its depth
And I'll be right there beside you, ready to step
Together we'll plunge
Down
Down
Down

Spotify Playlists

for when you're at the start of a relationship and your love language becomes sending people music

Spotify playlists have become a place that keeps displayed
the songs we've played and listened to –
there's no escaping *you.*

My history is filled with moments spent
content and lying in each other's arms,
phone passed eagerly between interlocked palms.
Tapping in titles,
artists and bands;
a way to understand each other,
expand one another's context
of where we came from
or what we've survived,
the lyrics and music that have soundtracked our lives
up until this very instant.

Instinctively
we start off tentative,
still attempting to give off
the impression we've got taste,
scared to face
the potential of seeming uncool,
ruling out songs we were into at school,
editing our guilty pleasures
to feel less guilty;
ultimately
I want you to still be into me.

Each melody leaves us more exposed.
I want you to show me what nobody knows.
I want you to show me the music you've grown with
so we can grow closer together.
Share the B-sides you love
beside me, under the covers.
Share with me your favourite covers.
Infiltrate my Spotify playlist,
make my daily mixes a reason to miss you daily
as they shuffle through the songs you've played me.

And they'll stay with me
for the rest of our time.
And if this should end, I'll keep them
and they'll become mine:
another song with a story
for someone else's Spotify.

As the World Falls Apart

We're falling in love
as the world falls apart.
Matters of the heart feel so minuscule
whilst the Earth burns in slow motion.
It's unnerving,
the notion that any moments of bliss
could exist alongside such terror.

I look into your eyes and there are explosions,
internally and externally.
I feel the need to hold on tight
as if there might be no tomorrow.

We're following a trajectory,
the outcome of which is perplexing.
Chaos is coming
and I'm becoming numb to the news;
it never ends.
I don't know where to begin
to try and make some sense.
So we orbit in our ignorance,
knowing any day this could be it.

And elsewhere
the streets are paved with nameless faces
just trying to keep pace
in a land that doesn't know, or care, that they exist.
Faith no longer satisfies
unless it's faith in empty lies
and eyes that have never seen what we've seen,
feet that have never stood where we've been.
We're after something tangible,
something we can hold,
like cash, or flesh, or drugs that numb,
to warm us from the cold that comes from simply *being.*

And elsewhere
the world is fleeing from itself,
feet pounding on ground;
I think that's how the Earth spins round these days,
powered by greed and fear.
And we're all here
watching as it happens,
thumbs sliding from one reel to another;
unable to uncover what is real or not anymore
and
unable to truly feel, we settle into numbness,
a sign that our humanity has slowly come undone.
It's the only way to place one foot in front of any other.
It's the only way to witness what we see and still recover.

Nothing matters.
Everything's war.
Wake up in the morning,
but what is it for?
Switch on the TV,
it's always the same:
ads that consume us
and people in pain.
Get on the tube
but nobody's there,
glued to their phones,
unable to care.

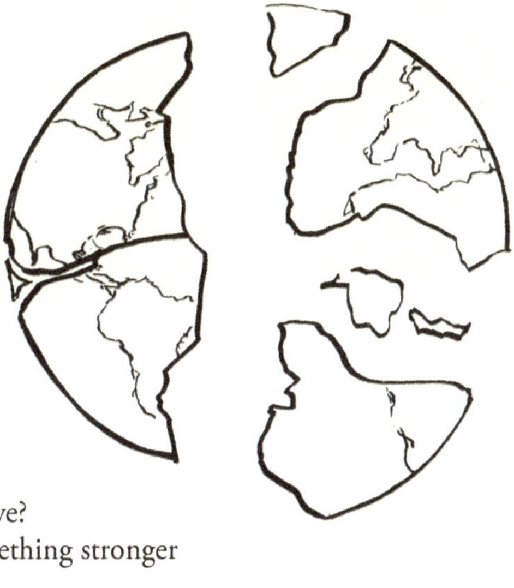

If lives are getting longer
why am I dying to feel alive?
Knock back coffee or something stronger
in order to survive.
There's something in the water,
we're all about to burst,
parched of real connection,
so much so we'll die of thirst.

It's palpable, this energy,
we're screaming into silence,
our lack of understanding
turns our desperance into violence.
We've capped off our compassion,
put a limit to our love,
extend it when it suits us,
tell ourselves we've done enough.
It hurts to be this numb.
Wound so tight we've come undone.
Consume to cover up the shame,
explain it's *just for fun.*

We're all running on empty,
though there's plenty to go round,
like crabs inside a barrel
trying to get to higher ground.
A pound won't get you far these days,
our heads are pounding from the maze
and constant blocks get in our way.
Are you okay?
Are you okay?
It seems a stupid thing to say.
Is anyone *okay* these days?
I'd be amazed.
It comes in waves.
You'll get your pay
another day,
another day.
We're running out of things to say.
Are you okay?
Are you okay?
Is this okay?

'Cause I don't want to be okay anymore
and I'm struggling to reason what all this is for.

So under covers I cling to you.
You are my constant in the fleeting.
You are the steady
grounding
beating.
And, for as long as we lie still,
can we still lie to ourselves
that we exist in insolation
from outside desperation?

And we'll persist
for moments stolen like this.
So let us bathe in this ever-fleeting sunshine
for as long as it has the audacity to glow.

Summer Dresses

Summer dresses, caps and shades
I always want to feel this way
The smell of suncream, hands on back
The sound of when the ice tray cracks
Your tapping fingers rest on thigh
The music plays, we breathe in sky
Me: laid with head upon your chest
This heat: the only way we rest
Blades of grass against my skin
Rearranging, pulling in
The hot car smell upon return
On naked skin the leather burns
You turn up volume, sing along
Not caring if our words are wrong
Wind down windows, elbows out
The little things: what life's about

The Mess

I did what I knew you couldn't
I left when I knew that you wouldn't
I said things I probably shouldn't
And oh, what a mess I have made

Worrying Is Like Suffering Twice

He said to me,
Worrying is like suffering twice,
and all the lights flickered
like he predicted my mind before it knew itself.
He said, *The trick is*
stay within the current
and the worries
will start to dissipate.

I complained I didn't know how,
that my brain was wired different somehow.
That staying was a struggle,
that my thoughts get in this muddle
and my mind works overdrive.
I try to ride it out,
but doubts and derisions
cloud decisions
and I lie awake at night
with the weight of everything
I've ever done,
am yet to do,
clawing at my skull beneath the sliver of the moon.
Sleep eludes me.
Nothing soothes me.
Rumination chews through me like an old dog with its toy.

And, as I tossed with my own toxicity,
his arms reached round the depths of me
and held me close.
He said,
Let go, succumb.
What is done can't be undone,
and what is yet to come
will happen whether you will it to or not.

He said,
I know you have magic within you,
but you cannot work miracles.
You cannot stop the passage of time,
and clinging on for dear life will only make your hands weary.
So rest, my love.
You have worked hard enough.
And the darkness drew in a little closer.

There is wonder in what is unseeable.
There is wisdom in what is unknowable.
You cannot slow the tides,
but you can learn to ride them out with patience.
Lie with me here
in the vastness of opportunity.
Right now, it's you and me,
and if you cannot rest here
you risk one day this moment disappearing.

And he pulled me in,
and there we stayed,
our bodies bent
like two commas taking pause
in a life that we'd been sentenced to,
our only power basking in the presence
of every word our next breaths drew,
and, foreheads touching,
we whispered sweet nothings
until the sun became the moon.

And outside, the beating city drummed at the window pane,
but inside, our stillness remained
untouched.

At least until the morning.
At least until the dawning of another daunting day.

You Let Your Insecurities

You let your insecurities get the best of you.
I swear it's true
that we would still be me and you
if you
could just let me be me.

You see,
you made your emotions my responsibility.
Placed your fragility
in my unconsenting hands.
The demands you made
on my time and energy
made of us enemies
without a remedy.

I craved serenity.
You craved the best of me
constantly, with constancy,
and so, despondently, I gave you all of me.
It cost me my agency,
which you disregarded flagrantly,
and brazenly
you made attempts at changing me,
rearranging me to suit you and fulfil your needs.

I long to be the character
you made up in your dreams,
the tantalising text you wrote and stuffed into the seams.
It seems
infantilising now,
this fantasised,
idealised
pixie dream you brought to life.
I suffocate on your creation.
She bears no weight

and no relation
to the beta source.
Things were going well until
she knocked me off my course.

Of course, I wish to be more like her:
carefree,
sexy,
up for fucking constantly.
It's a fucking contradiction,
this friction I feel
of not comparing to your picture,
the curse of being real,
multifaceted and richer.

I poured my sense of self away.
I edited the things I say
in some attempt to satiate,
in order not to complicate
or contradict.
Constantly considering
how best to sidestep conflict.
Attempting to predict
at least twelve steps ahead,
possible reactions
always running through my head
and so instead
I bit my tongue.
I think I chewed so hard
I didn't know where it had gone.
And for too long
I shrank away,
so scared of getting lost
I almost think that's why I stayed.

I need some time.
I need some space.
I need to find the *me* erased.

Retrace my steps.
Replace the parts I should have kept
but let myself lose.

I had to choose:
my integrity or
you
made me doubt my own reality
and shout,
insanity that I could do without.

And in your place
there will be space and vacancy.
There will be pain,
and occasionally
there will be moments where I hate myself,
berating the weight of the decision I've taken.

But I have taken it.
Me.
I have set myself free.

And you will see
that there is no such thing as one-way liberation.
You are free to live the life of your creation,
the one dreamt up
in that beautiful imagination of yours.

And of course
my heart is broken.
But at least it's not my mind.
At least it's not the spirit of the girl I left behind.
I will find her again.
It's true.
For she needs everything
but you.

She Dances

for Norah

a poem about refinding yourself after a relationship, specifically on the dance floor

She dances in shoes
that clip-clop like wild horses on shores.
Reclaiming herself like never before.
She's fought many battles,
and stamping her feet on the ground is the sound of the triumph
that here she still stands.

Many have planned her demise.
She moves through the air as an act of revival.
Taking up space is her fight for survival.
She's thriving
in a way I've never seen
and in this moment
dances every version that has been.
The past and the future.
The music moves through her,
igniting through motion a glorious scene.

The rhythm, it bends to her will,
for she will not be bent anymore.
A fire is burning
and she is now learning
to nourish herself right down to her core.

There is so much more to her
than meets the eye.
There's beauty in her
no money can buy.
And, try as we might,
those who cling to her tight
need reminding she was never ours to contain.

For she is the sun, the giver of life,
we mortals transfixed as we bathe in her light.

It can be frightening
to fall so completely
for the wildest of things,
to trust and let go,
allow them to grow
and to bloom.

And here in this room,
as she holds us all so captive,
it's as if all paths have led her to this
and she has found herself
exactly where she's meant to be,
dancing out demons to set herself free.

And we
get to watch her
blossom in our presence,
get to witness her,
at her most present,
present us with her gift.

And as she shifts from side to side
I see how the weight of the world it subsides
and, like the tides,
how they ebb and flow on the sand,
she's learning to breathe and let go, yet still stand,
more brilliant,
more resilient
and more powerful
than ever before.

Hackney Street

in a city of almost 9 million people, it feels pretty mad to cross paths with someone you used to know

When I see you on some Hackney street,
a part of me, it feels complete.
Seasons have passed since I last knew your presence,
my reasons for leaving are losing their resonance,
and in the pleasantries exchanged
I wish this moment would remain
unaltered by the reality
of a life without each other.

And I wish that I could say

that I smoke cigarettes
to remind me of the taste of you,
tobacco trails that shed from you,
the clues that always led to you
blown away now in the wind.

That I endure the taste I used to hate
because it means a hit of a moment spent with you,
huddled outside of nightclubs
shouting into each other's ears
our vibrant, heightened hopes and fears
or sitting drinking coffee
in our favourite weekend cafés,
feeling far more continental
than a girl from Oldham ever should.

That I go to sleep
to dream of you,
to walk through violet fields with you,
to talk in the surreal with you
until the morning comes.
That I shut myself away and lie
in wait of impending tranquillity
for it might bring you back to me
even for a fleeting moment.
It's strange for me to think
that one day I'll have known you through my portal of slumber
far longer than the actual number of days
I knew you in the mortal world.

Everything is morphed now.
Memories have missing moments.
The mundane in its haze feels like something amazing
I'm afraid I gave up too easily on.

And I have searched for you in strangers' faces
in the hope that they would help replace
the ease with which I fell in love with you.

I've listened to a lover laugh
and cursed your name when mine falls flat
because no one quite has ways with words like you do.

I've kissed them with desire,
something full and so entire,
as if my lips could will you back here to this sofa in my house.
As if our mouths themselves were portals,
as if we weren't just merely mortals
moving on together, separately,
with cracks within our hearts.

So when I see you on some Hackney street
it's no surprise it makes me feel complete,
for there's a piece of me you've taken,
forged with love and some mistakes,
and in the moments where you hate me
I hope it brings you comfort too:

I simply haven't found the thing
I had when spent with you.

No Grave

It's strange
To have no grave that we can visit
No flowers we can lay
Yet I will tend to the rose in my glasses
For at least when they are watered
And no matter how distorted
I can keep my tether back to you
Even if their stems are skewed

The truth is
I'd rather picture you
In all of your nostalgic glory
Than regretfully acknowledge
All the petals
As they fall upon the countertop
You still love me
You love me not

I wish that you had died sometimes
I think it's human nature
Better you were taken than accept your slow erasure
Better a full stop
Than this most torturous ellipsis
You're gone to me but still exist
My world stands still
But you persist

Why Did You Stay?

a poem commissioned by the charity Refuge to open their Red Flags campaign for International Women's Day, raising awareness of the lesser-known forms of domestic abuse

the campaign included an immersive installation that featured hundreds of physical red flags, each displaying a quote from a domestic abuse survivor, and a soundscape featuring actors' voices reading powerful renditions of survivors' words

the public were invited to wander round the space, to read the red flags and to share and reflect

Why did you stay?

they say,
as if I've never heard that question,
as if it's not the thing that leaves my lips
when met with my reflection,
for my perception of myself is skewed;
I don't know how I got there.
It's not the life for me I'd choose, but somehow I got lost there.

So why did I stay?

Because the warning signs were subtle.
I knew to look for danger, for the violent signs of trouble,
so yeah, I struggled to see the smaller signs,
to read between the blurring lines,
and by the time I realised
it was already getting too late.

So why did I stay?

Because it's a chipping away;
you notice a crack, not a quiet decay.

And it started so good,
like these things often do,
and you're falling in love and it's shiny and new,
and you overlook the little things, the moments when they criticise;
you tell yourself, to be in love, it's all about the compromise.
So you alter your behaviour
if it helps them feel more stable;
you see them and they're struggling,
but you are strong and able,
so if a few more texts when out with friends would bring them peace,
that's not too far a stretch if it enables some relief.

So why stay?

They say if you put a frog in boiling water
it saves itself immediately,
but put it into cold and slowly heat it:
unbelievably
the frog, it won't perceive as gradually the heat increases,
and so it intensifies
until the poor frog is deceased.

You see,
it starts off small.
So small you think you've got it handled.
Until you're feeling overwhelmed
by the sheer weight of their demands
and you understand that they're in pain
and you understand that you're the cause
and you understand that if you change
things can return to like before,
and all you wanted was to love them,
all you wanted was to please,
and if you edit your behaviour maybe this can be achieved.
So you'll leave the party early
or perhaps not go at all;
you'll keep your phone in sight so you can be at beck and call.
And all you need to do is keep things light;

if you just behave, you'll be alright
on this tightrope where you're balancing
whilst all around's unravelling
and with each tip of toe
all you have is the hope
that you can make it through to one more day.

So why stay?

It's hard to see the red flags when your glass is tinted rose
and it's hard to choose yourself when seeking love is what we're sold.

So why did you stay?

Maybe we need to stop and reframe the question,
for perhaps the answer lies inside the tone of its suggestion.
The emphasis is put on me, the blame insinuated.
It's because I blamed myself that I stayed stuck in situations,
and the shame you feel,
the shame, it cuts you off from all you know.
Withdrawing from your loved ones, leaving nowhere else to go,
and you're looking in a mirror at a face you can't recall.
You can't believe they want someone
so pathetic and so small.

So no,
please don't ask me
why it was that I stayed.
A better question we must ask
is ***why did they…?***

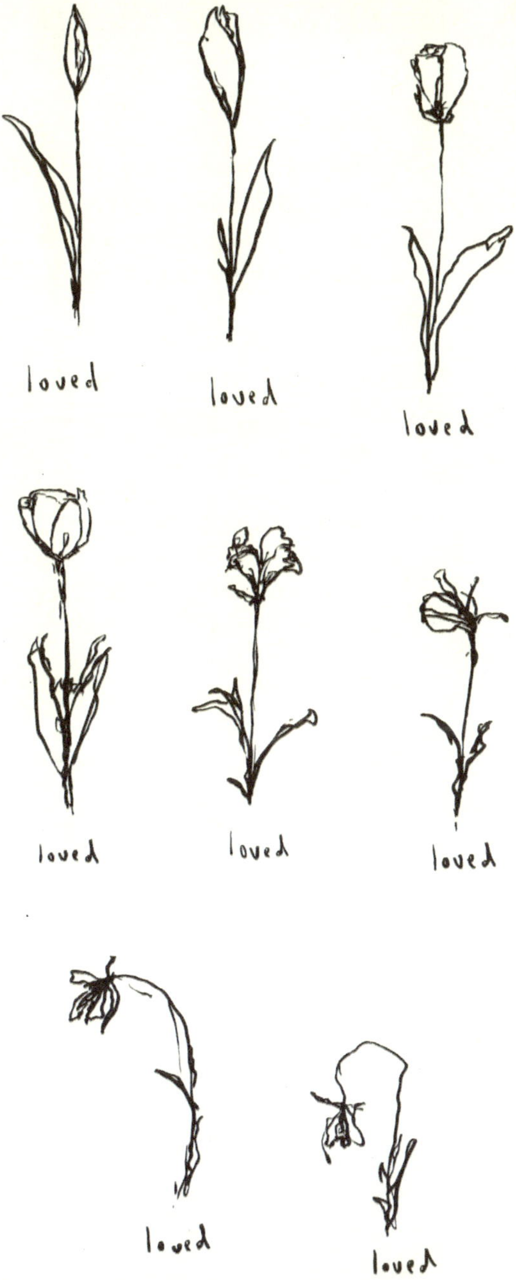
loved
loved
loved
loved
loved
loved
loved
loved

Home Is Where the Heart Is

for Sammy

They say that home is where the heart is
But I think I disagree
I'd say your heart is where your home is
And in your heart we all will be

For love creates foundations
And on that base we build a home
If the bricks are those who've loved you
Then you'll never be alone

So no matter your location
Or the life that you pursue
You can't leave home behind
Because that home is built in you

At What Point

a poem that I wrote in my bedroom in the midst of despair
that has resonated with thousands and has given me hope

At what point
do you tell a girl
a park's not just for play?
At nighttime stay away.
There's danger lurking all around,
and round about dusk
the rustles in the bushes might be home to something
much more menacing
than bushy-tailed creatures
that are out to steal your crisps.
The risks of a shortcut.

I bet you Uber's kept afloat
out of women's pockets,
makes its profits
as the cons of walking home alone
far outweigh the pros.
And does she know
that she'll pay for a taxi to avoid getting murdered by a stranger,
then spend the entire journey aware of the danger
that *this* might be the stranger
who will finally murder her?

If I had a pound
for all the pounds lost
due to the cost of having to consider
getting home without accostment
I still wouldn't earn the same as men.
But then again
the system's rigged to constantly remind us
our beauty is behind us
and so we must invest

in lotions and potions, the extent of the ocean,
to maintain a sense of relevance.

I'm relatively sure
if I had saved all the money
that promised flatter tummies
or younger skin
or looking thin
or better hair
or buying uncomfortable underwear
for him
for him
for him
I'd be halfway to a mortgage.
But, more than that,
I'd have a sense of power back.

They profit off our lack, you see.
Attack appearance constantly.
Confine us to the binary
of slut or saint.
We can't escape, but both are tainted.
We're well acquainted with the shame,
born into a losing game.

And it's the same with contraception.
Sex is no exception.
We're expected to bear the burden
or else bear a birth that we never expected,
hadn't projected for.
And, if we're lucky enough to get the pill for free,
the bill will be floated by our bloated bodies
and it could cost us anything
from mood swings and low sex drive
to blood clots and higher rates of suicidal thoughts and depression.
It's giving the impression
that we expect this as par for the course of 'womanhood',

but it is understood
that we would never accept this for a man,
and who would trust them anyway?

So, we'll pay more to conform
to societal norms,
even down to spending more on our school uniforms.
Twelve percent more for a girl's blazer.
Not to mention on tampons and razors.
It's crazy
but so normalised that it used to not faze me.

Sometimes I wonder who I'd be
if I existed just for me.
If my entire existence hadn't consisted
of persistently viewing myself through a male's gaze.
If the haze lifted
and I could wear whatever the fuck I want without consequence.
And yet, I'm well aware
of the hypocrisy of getting older.
I'm well aware that not too far from now
their looks I once despised I'll begin to crave.
It's exposing in their light but so much colder in their shade.

If a woman falls in a forest and there's no man there to save her,
can she even say she lived at all?

I dread the moment I might feel invisible,
when my aging body is less considerable.
No wonder people are getting surgery to feel less fucking miserable.

Do you know how it feels to hover above yourself?
Hyperaware.
The left foot in the present,
the right not really there because it's running away with itself,
preparing itself for what could possibly go wrong
because it *has* gone wrong.

I'm tired of constant vigilance.
I'm tired of constant vigils.
They seem to be rising
without uprising
and yet we act surprised every time
another woman gets killed.
Don't be too nice
it could get you killed.
Don't be so rude
it could get you killed.
Socialised into a politeness
that still
gets us
killed.

They rap *bitch* at us and yet within the same breath
complain they're not getting enough respect.
And it's reflected in real life.
It's reflected in 'banter' with the guys.
It's reflected in the wage gap.
The thigh gap.
The orgasm gap.
The fact that victims are rarely believed.
The fact that justice is barely achieved.
The fact that it costs us so much more
to just *be.*

So tell me,
because I want to hear what you have to say for it:

At what point do you tell your girl
her life is only worth what she is able to pay for it?

Risk it or uber?
male gaze
Saint or slut?
Anti age

'It Is Not for Us to Have Shame; It Is Them'

– Gisèle Pelicot

On the greyness of the tube
I look up
and catch the eyes of an older woman staring back.
Heavy wrinkles map her face,
proof of all the places and the people
that caused impact.

Some deeper than the others, unexpected, more profound.
And I can read between the lines of all her smiles and all her frowns.
Study all the memories engraved upon her face,
the path that she has forged through the most difficult of days.
Her gaze, it never falters,
body language never alters.
An open book,
welcoming me to take a look.

See me, she implies.
I exist and I've survived,
and so will you
and so will she.
Don't you dare avert your eyes.

And then she smiles
and I smile back.
And then our smiles begin to crack
into a grin
and all the while her son wants in
but can't begin to understand.

We laugh at the absurdity.
We're laughing now with urgency,
so fervently.
As if our laughter is the sound
of all the women they have silenced.
As if our laughter is in answer
to their actions, which are violence.
As if our laughter is the only thing
to plaster all the pain they bring
and turn it into something sweet.
For isn't that our power?

When she gets off the tube there is silence so deafening,
but what remains in her wake is defiance and reckoning.

a poem commissioned by Amnesty International UK and Shangri-La for Glastonbury 2025

Amnesty International UK and Shangri-La joined forces to create an artistic activation in order to honour and amplify the ongoing fight for women's rights and equality

alongside my poem, the activation included an interactive tree sculpture that invited festivalgoers to add their own messages of resistance and solidarity with women worldwide

the aim was to inspire hope, defiance and empowerment while challenging all individuals to recognise their role in continuing to fight for women's rights

Threads of Resistance

Your body holds the history of every generation that came before it;
you cannot ignore it
or drown out its existence –
for *you* are the resistance.
And their persistence to be seen and heard,
to fight for lives we so deserve,
runs deep within your veins;
the threads of them remain.

For we are woven out of women's labour,
the rights they fought for, the life they gave us,
and they paved the way for change that we so often take for
granted;
we feast on fruit from trees born out of seeds that they have
planted.

And we are tethered to each other.
We're your sisters, we're your mothers,
so, if one of us is struggling, that thread will feel the strain;
location does not matter
for our fight is still the same.

There's some that want to block our path,
stop our progress in its tracks;
attacking our autonomy,
they view us as commodities,
an oddity for them to scapegoat and to blame –
they cut away our rights, but our resilience remains.

So they bombard us with minutiae
to occupy our minds,
use distraction as a tactic
to keep us all confined,
but, much like Mother Earth,
how she still spins whilst they assault her,
our strength within ourselves,
what we hold true will never falter.

And they might trick us into thinking
we're each other's competition;
that's the perfect definition of divide and conquer –
for what could be stronger
than women, versed in empathy,
turning that towards each other;
than women, with integrity,
helping uplift one another?

You see, our bodies hold the history
of every generation that came before us.
You cannot ignore us.
You will not ignore us.
Stand with us and for us
now –
this is your moment
to show what you're composed of:

does your allyship hold true
or is it easily disposed of?

Yet Again

Yet again
Our lives are in the hands of men
Who weren't told enough
That they were loved as children

Now We Know

We're out of gas
We're out of steam
We're giving up
On all our dreams
Of better days
And safer nights
Of moving left
Instead of right
Of looking up
To clearer skies
Of breathing in
Our cleaner sighs
Of fewer lies

A woman cries
From joy alone
No longer scared
Of walking home
A black man kneels
To share his love
No longer protesting the glove
That holds him down

A dusty town
Begins to thrive
Return the people
Who've survived
A child plays
Out in the street
Waves at the strangers that she meets

And all the trees
Begin to grow
And what was fast
Begins to slow
And now we *know*
We take our time

No longer ignoring
The signs
What's yours is mine
And mine is yours
We each have keys
To all the doors

There are no more wars
On stolen land
There are no more people
Who are banned
For crossing lines
We never owned
There are no more children
On their own
In little boats
Sailing away
Dinghies are only used for play

We have a say
In how it's spent
We all become
The one percent

The climate cools
The sea subsides
No longer fearing
Genocide
We look inside
Into our minds
Challenge the biases we find

We open up
There's no more shame
Men learn to cry
And love again
We master strength
It's something soft
Sincerity
Should not be crossed

We're all for one
And one for all
We realise life
Is in the small
It's in the moments with a friend
It's when the music never ends
It's in the way they hold you tight
It's in the way you sleep at night
With no more pain
With no more stress
We are content
With having less

But I digress
We ask too much
They say *let go of that you clutch*
They say *move on*
They say *no more*
They say *there's danger on the shore*
In people form

They say they've warned us of the threat
They promise things they then forget
And so we sweat for better lives
And so we cling on to their lies
And we're surprised
They let us down
And we're surprised
They turn around
On what they say
On what they owe

But *now we know*
Yes, *now we know*

Questions to My Conscience

it is incredibly easy to become numb to the news and to the atrocities we are witnessing on social media every single day. I don't want to become numb in the face of marginalised groups having their rights stripped away and a genocide that is being livestreamed to our palms

I wrote these questions in an attempt to hold myself accountable

How much capacity
Do you have for tragedy?
Or are you getting so numb
That it's losing the gravity?

How much more space
Can you give to the rage
Till it gets so consuming
You choose not to engage?

How many more fucks
Can you practically give
About strangers unknown
Who are fighting to live?

Is your image worth more
Than the things you abhor?
You claimed you'd never be complicit
Now you're feeling less sure

If you post but don't oppose
Are your politics for show?

Are you weary?
Are you wary?
Is it all too fucking scary?
Are you getting tired of caring?

Are you muting out the blaring?
Is it tearing you apart
Or you don't know where to start?

Find your heart
Find your humanity
Hold your own through this depravity

If you're seeing something
Shout it
Put your money where your mouth is
This is more than you and likes
This is basic human rights

Say it with your chest
Don't wait for something else
To come along that's even worse
This is not some first rehearsal

Violence breeds violence
It sleeps in our silence
It rests and restores
And returns more deplorable

Use your voice for those who can't
Use your voice because you still can

Hold on to your integrity
Nurture it authentically
Because eventually
You will be asked

Who are you?
What is it that you stand for?

I hope to God you know the answer

Much Greater

With divisions they are stronger
Hate and anger their creators
But with love and hope and kindness
We will always be much greater

Gin & Platonic

for the loves of my life: my friends x

Pour me a gin
for I'm needing some tonic.
To be honest,
I can live without the gin;
I just need someone to fill my cup,
and you've always been so good at that.

Time with you is dipping toes in blue
and lapping up language.
You make the vague something tangible.
You make the daunting more manageable.
And over cups of tea
or shitty TV
we've dragged ourself out of our mid-twenties,
emerging mostly unscathed.

Like sun-kissed divorcees
smoking cigarettes,
caution to the wind with their regrets,
indulging one another,
absolving the other of sins,
we sink into our skin,
shaking off the insecurity of youth
yet remaining for the other, proof
and witness
of what brought us here before.

To be known and loved.
To be seen and understood.
To truly feel enough.

When we talk of life's love stories
we will talk of romance and meet-cutes,
club meets and reboots,
the kisses and missed connections,
the toughest of rejections,
the heartbreaks and butterflies,
the one-night stands
before we meet the one who stands
the test of time,
and that's all fine,
but I wonder…

Will we talk of this?
Will we speak of us?
Will we romanticise platonic love?
Pay homage to the humble,
the ones who stumbled alongside all the highs and lows
and misdemeanours,
gave meaning to our madness
and held us in the absence of any other kind of love;
will just friendship be enough?

Sure, sex is great,
but laughing with your mates over something trivial?
Is biblical.
It is gifted by the gods.

So
pour me that gin,
or whatever it is you have lying around.
It's really not about the gin
(I don't even like gin).
It's about us,
taking the time to drink each other in,
savouring this platonic love.

For it is the elixir
far better than any spirit or mixer.
And as we sit and sip and reminisce
I want us to always remember this:

This is the moment.
This the destination.
This the greatest love story
that will always bring salvation.

Hey, You're Okay

for you

Hey,
you're okay.
I know it feels like life might be rolling away,
but come back to yourself.
Stay strong.
The beauty of life is in getting things wrong.
We're not long for this world,
you and I.
Better to end having everything tried
than die trying to scrape back the time,
rifling through what-could-have-beens in our mind.

Hey,
you're alright.
I know that it feels like you're caught in a fight.
Sometimes it's outwards but mostly within;
there's a war going on and it's under your skin.
I see you're in pain;
I understand.
Life hasn't gone quite the way you had planned,
but come back to yourself;
stay strong.
It may be that this was the plan all along.

Hey,
this will pass.
I know that this feels like the wake of a blast.
I know that there's anger,
I know that there's shame
and so many feelings you're struggling to name.
I know that you're running and don't know what from.
I know that there's days when you wish there were none,

and gone is the freedom that you used to feel;
drifting through life's slowly lost its appeal.
There's a realness now to the choices you make,
a more human cost if you make a mistake.
You're dancing on eggshells,
coughing up smoke,
deflecting questions with diverting jokes.
You're screaming for change but you can't quite create it,
stifled by life but so scared to detonate it.

You're awaiting something,
but you don't know quite what.
You had it once,
but by now you've forgot.
It's a lot;
it's almost too much to hold.
You're searching for *something* to make you feel whole
or feel held,
and in the quiet of night, where your body once melded to another,
you lie awake remembering all the lovers that you could've
or you should've or you would've
if life had gone a different way.
You play out all the means by which
you might have made them stay,
if just for one more measly moment,
one more mediocre day.

But please, hold on.
Please hold your nerve.
Don't you dare fucking settle for less than you deserve.
You are loved.
You're not alone.
In this space you have a home,
in this place where people meet
just to hear another speak
some words of comfort or connection.

A place of laughter and reflection.
A place of rage and introspection.
Where every single person here
has overcome rejection
or is dealing with it now.

If you'll allow,
let us hold your imperfections
for a portion of the evening,
and take the deepest breath
just to remind yourself you're breathing;
let *this* be a part of healing.
And know that everything you're feeling,
someone else has felt it too.
Let the darkest part of others
shine a light inside of you.

You've been so strong
and in this moment here, right now,
you've found where you belong.

The Sun Will Rise

The sun will rise
The sun will set
Sometimes it's easy to forget
That there is beauty in this world, and yet
The sun will rise
The sun will set
And I will love you
As surely as the days turn into night
As surely as the dark becomes the light
And colours bleed
Throughout the sky
And flowers bloom, then wilt, then die
As surely as the passages of time
This love I hold will never misalign
And so
If nothing else
Please know that someone else has truly loved you
And so
If nothing else
Please know, when all else ends
That there was love

Acknowledgements

It takes a village to create a Spoken Word poet.

Thank you to the London spoken word scene for being my tether in an overwhelming, anonymous city. You have given me community, a space to process and heal, and endless inspiration.

Thank you specifically to the hosts and organisers of events who saw something in me and have given me opportunities. Nothing beats the feeling of getting paid (however small) for something you wrote in your bedroom. I'm going to shout out some nights here but please know I am only scratching the surface of what London has to offer:

Henry Beckwith (aka Ted Temple) & Groove Verse – finding your podcast 'Word Spoken' during Covid encouraged me to start writing again. Attending Groove Verse after lockdown blew me away and gave me something to strive for. Thank you for being an amazing pal and advocate for poetry.

Jenny Foulds & Rebel Soapbox – thank you for giving me my first ever open mic opportunity. If it had gone terribly, I quite possibly would never have touched a mic again.

Memo Brown & Says Events – thank you for giving me and so many others our first paid(!) headline gigs.

Casey Arturo & Poet's Palace – thank you for the encouragement, opportunities and laughs.

The VERSES boys, Jak, Nash & Natz – thank you for taking me to the Roundhouse with you and for being one of the most warm and welcoming nights on the scene.

The Writer's Block team, Woodzy, Fury, Y.A, Simon, – you give us all something to aspire to.

There are so many other brilliant nights and poets, far too many to mention and probably one for every night of the week if you needed. (Do yourself a favour and get searching some of them.) Thank you to anyone I haven't mentioned who has given me a space in your room or on your mic.

To my SpitNights team, Danny Mash, Celine Kutevu, Georgie Cahill, Sam Thomson, April Spiers and Emy Dentler – what we are creating is something beautiful and necessary. Thank you for letting me join your gang and for platforming poetry in a meaningful way. Thank you for being a place of constant support and advice. This is only the beginning.

A second shoutout to Emy for being the organised, bad German bitch this disorganised lil creative needs to achieve her visions.

And once again, to Danny Mash. Thank you for the opportunities, the suitcases, the hours spent editing captions on reels and for being a great social secretary.

Thank you, Harry Baker and Georgie Jones. Two of my favourite poets and kindest people. Thank you for all of the advice and opportunities, you make a life in poetry feel achievable. Thank you for helping me navigate confusing commission conversations when it feels baffling that anyone would want to pay you for words that come out of your head.

Thank you, Bradley Taylor, for being my new favourite poet and for listening to my book anxieties. Every time I watch you, you blow me away and make me strive to be better.

Thank you, Clive and Kate Birnie, for trusting in me and my work enough to publish my debut book. *Burning Eye* was my dream publisher, ever since I read Leyla Josephine's beautiful collection. Thank you again, Harry Baker, for putting us in contact and allowing that dream to become a reality. Meeting you both has been a pleasure start to finish and the support you have given throughout has kept me on the right side of overwhelm.

Thank you, Harriet Evans, for editing this book with the lightest of touch and for the considerate back and forth that led to better punctuation and, most definitely, a better book.

Thank you, Emily Treloar, for your beautiful illustrations. You were the first person to read a draft of this book and your beautiful work has elevated it far beyond what I could have hoped for. Don't talk to strangers unless they're doodling in a café and you think they look really cool.

And now closer to home.

Thank you, Sarah Nelson, James Atherton and Craig Harris. Thank you for making a creative life feel achievable for a group of kids from Oldham. Thank you for instilling us with confidence, excellent politics and for allowing us a voice. You taught us discipline, self-belief and how to tell a great story.

Thank you to all of my OTW fam and alumni.

Sarah, you are the reason I wrote my first poem. You saw something in me and I can never thank you enough for your support, advice and unwavering belief over these years. Thank you for introducing me to Hollie McNish via YouTube and thus proving to me that poetry can be cool, political and relatable.

Thank you, Norah Lopez Holden, for everything. You have lived alongside me and the content of these poems. Without you I'd have been lost. You are the best momager.

Katie, Amber, Sammy and Emily - the friendship you have given me is the one I will write odes about for the rest of my life. Thank you for the laughs, the tears, the advice, the support, the phone calls and the sympathetic cheers in the audience when no one else seemed to be getting the joke. Thank you for healing several of my broken hearts and for being my touchstone on reality.

Katie Pickering, thank you for your embroidery skills that have made the cover of this book as beautiful as it is. Thank you for being my rock for 7 years and for being my home in London.

Thank you, Mia, for the nourishment, both literal and spiritual. You have soothed me during this hectic period.

Jake, Lewis, Oli, Joe, Tim, Chris – thank you for the laughs and showing me that good, kind men truly do exist.

Thank you, Jack Garratt, for being a creative soundboard and for your honest encouragement. I'm so glad I pretended to not know who you were in that bar a year ago. Thank you also Tamzene.

Thank you, Abraham Popoola, for the conversations that enriched me as a creative, a friend and a human. Even though you're miles away, I will always hold them close.

Thank you, Ant Hickman, creating a podcast with you and meeting beautiful creatives through it has kept me sane in my lowest moments. (It's called **'Have You Got Your Sh*t Together?'** and yes, that is a plug.)

Thank you to any friend I have dragged along with me to a random open mic night 70 minutes away from where you live. The beautiful thing about poetry is that you never know who you'll meet or where you'll end up.

Thank you to my Outlander family and to the most loyal fans who welcomed me in and have encouraged and shared my poetic journey.

Thank you, John Bell, for the road trips and magical adventures.

To the people who have broken my heart and whose hearts I have broken – thank you for our time together, no matter how imperfect. I think we both tried. It's really fucking hard. Thank you for trying to love me in the ways that you knew how. I write poems to process my own feelings but I'm aware that there are two sides to every relationship and I'm sure I provided my fair share of content. Thank you for helping me learn how to love better.

Thank you to my therapists. God bless the NHS.

Thank you to my family. The Irish and the English, the Northern and the Southern. Thank you for indulging my living room performances and for raising me with good morals and secure love.

Mum, thank you for your kindness, your tenacity and your strong sense of justice.

Dad, thank you for your tenderness, your ability to listen, your childlike joy and for all of the lifts (I would learn to drive but then when would we have our catch ups?)

Sis, thank you for your fierce loyalty, your strength and your encouragement. Thank you for being the chalk to my overly emotional cheese. You are the strongest person I know.

And finally, thanks to YOU. Thank you for buying/ borrowing/ stumbling across this book. Thanks for reading. Thanks for coming to my gigs. Thanks for sharing my work and relating to the things I write. Thank you for making me feel like there are other people out there who might also think the same as me.

Thank you for showing me

You are not alone, I also feel this.

www.ingramcontent.com/pod-product-compliance
Lightning Source LLC
LaVergne TN
LVHW090856100726
842905LV00054B/404
* 9 7 8 1 9 1 3 9 5 8 5 0 3 *